Plays for Puppets

Based on well-known fairy tales adaptable for stage production

Roy Wilkinson

Rudolf Steiner College Press

This publication was made possible by a grant from
The Waldorf Curriculum Fund.

The name Waldorf really belongs only to the first school of its type, the one founded by Rudolf Steiner in Stuttgart, Germany for the children of the workers at the Waldorf-Astoria factory. It has since been adopted as the generic name of schools conducted according to Rudolf Steiner's recommendations. In place of Waldorf some establishments call themselves Rudolf Steiner schools. Others take a distinctive name and add Waldorf or Rudolf Steiner in some connection as a subtitle.

First published by E. J. Arnold & Son, Ltd., Leeds, 1957

Reprinted 1993 by Rudolf Steiner College Press

ISBN 0-945803-65-6

Rudolf Steiner College Press
9200 Fair Oaks Blvd.
Fair Oaks, CA 95628, U.S.A.

CONTENTS

PREFACE

These plays have a story. For some years I taught in the north of England at a Rudolf Steiner school where foreign languages are introduced into the early classes, even into the Nursery. The children make their first acquaintance with the language by means of the spoken word, phrases, songs, poems and miming. In this connection it occurred to me that puppets might be useful. Early training in stagecraft proved an undoubted asset. I made a few glove puppets and tried out a version of "The Frog Prince" in German. The result was astonishing. The class of five and six-year-olds listened very intently and apparently with complete understanding. Had the language been Hottentot or Chinese I am sure they would have listened equally well.

A friend suggested starting a Puppet Theatre and we immediately set to work. Apart from the language work in school we were anxious that it should be educational as well as entertaining, and the obvious choice of material was the old fairy tales and legends with their intrinsic wisdom.

No sooner had we a small repertoire in hand than we were engaged by the Leeds Corporation to give performances during the summer in the parks — hence the setting of "The Travelling Musicians". There followed engagements at schools, hospitals, orphanages, parties, even at homes of rest for the aged.

After one such engagement I was approached by the representative of a well-known firm of publishers with the request to see a script of the plays with a view to publication. Unfortunately it did not exist or only sketchily so. For the greater part we had made up the text as we went along although it had gradually become fixed and, in several cases, had fallen into some sort of rhyme. So I had to sit down and compose. This is how these plays came to be "written".

They were duly submitted to the publisher and I was called to an interview. Among other complimentary remarks made by the editor one struck me as showing great insight and perception — "These plays were not written, they were acted". How true!

They were published in due course; the edition was sold out and the copyright reverted to the author. As friends and colleagues still ask for them, it was decided to reprint. Hence the present edition.

As in the original, a few stage directions and diagrams have been included in the text as a guide but producers are free to improve on these. Perhaps a word of explanation about the diagrams is necessary. These are drawn as if looking towards the audience. They show the hands used for the puppets and relative positions. If four puppets are shown on one diagram it does not necessarily mean that all four are appearing at once. Reference to the text will make this clear. The puppets actually acting can range at will.

Most of these plays can be produced by two manipulators but an assistant is useful on occasion.

One of the secrets of successful puppet play production is to get the audience to join in. There are numerous instances in these plays where this is possible. They are usually indicated by the word "backchat". Here is an opportunity for the puppeteer to use his own wit and intelligence to exploit the situation.

The directions given are for producing the plays with puppets but they also lend themselves to production in the ordinary way and can be adapted for use with larger groups as, for instance, in schools.

The problem in producing plays with a class of children is that all must be accommodated and not all children are natural actors. One usually needs therefore a few leading parts, many minor ones and some crowd scenes. Most of the plays here can be adapted and extra characters can even be introduced. For instance, in "The Owl", the burgomaster could have attendants and a crowd could gather to watch the proceedings and perhaps add encouraging remarks. In "Rumpelstiltskin", both king and queen could also have attendants. There can be wayfarers in "The Travelling Musicians" with whom the donkey passes the time of day and a whole crowd of robbers. Crowd scenes are also feasible in both "The Dragon and the Boy with the Flute" and "The Donkey, the Table and the Stick".

Roy Wilkinson

THE BILLY GOATS GRUFF

(*Acting time 20 minutes*)

CHARACTERS

GREAT BIG BILLY GOAT GRUFF
BIG BILLY GOAT GRUFF
LITTLE BILLY GOAT GRUFF
MONSTER

This is a well-loved and favourite play with children, which is very easy to perform. There are the three goats (made in three sizes) and the monster. The only other property required is the bridge, which can be indicated by a kind of balustrade made of wood.

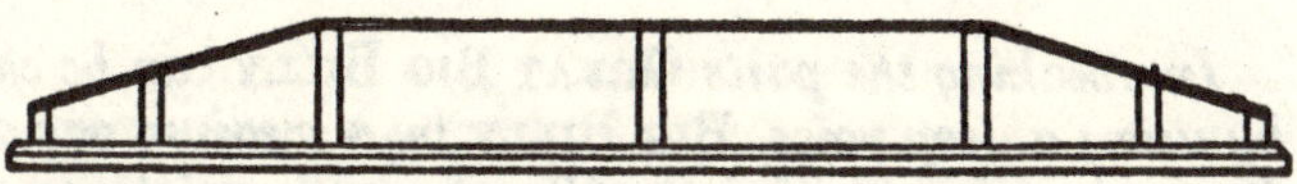

The monster can be as ingenious as the maker fancies. The original one had a distorted human face, two horns and red hair.

PUPPET POSITIONS FOR SCENE I

MELODY FOR OPENING AND CLOSING CHORUS

In speaking the parts GREAT BIG BILLY *can be characterized by using a deep voice,* BIG BILLY *by a medium one and* LITTLE BILLY *by a shrill piping. All notes and variations can be used for the* MONSTER.

SCENE I

THE THREE GOATS *sing.*

We are the Billy Goats Gruff,
We are the Billy Goats Gruff,
We are Bill, Bill, Billy Goats Gruff,
We are the Billy Goats Gruff.

GREAT BIG BILLY [*singing*].

I am the Great Big Billy Goat Gruff,
etc.

BIG BILLY [*singing*].

I am the big Billy Goat Gruff,
etc.

LITTLE BILLY [*singing*].

I am the little Billy Goat Gruff,
etc.

ALL THREE [*singing*].

We are the Billy Goats Gruff,
etc.

GREAT BIG BILLY [*turning to the others*].

Brothers Gruff, brothers Gruff,
Of food up here there's not enough.
I'm hungry and I want to eat,
Scarce can I stand upon my feet.

BIG BILLY [*turning first to one, then the other*].

You are not the only one.
Nearly all my strength is gone.
I'm empty and I want a meal.
You've no idea how bad I feel.

LITTLE BILLY [*turning to the others*].

You two are big and fat and strong,
But I can hardly get along.
Brothers Gruff, I've got so thin,
My ribs are sticking through my skin.

GREAT BIG BILLY.

All the grass is eaten here,
We must search elsewhere, that's clear.
We need some food ; where can we go ?
That's a thing I'd like to know.

BIG BILLY.

True enough we must move on,
All the food from here is gone.
There's not enough to feed a fly,
We must find some food or die.
[*Supports himself on* GREAT BIG BILLY.]

LITTLE BILLY.

Yes, let us go away from here,
If we stop we starve, I fear.
If much longer here I stay,
I shall simply waste away.

GREAT BIG BILLY [*pointing*].

Across the river there is food,
Rich and plentiful and good.
If we could once get over there,
We should be rid of all this care.

BIG BILLY.

Yes, there the grass is fresh and sweet,
For us a long-awaited treat.
There are some fruits and berries too.
If only now I had a few!

LITTLE BILLY.

Across the river all is green,
And good red apples have I seen.
To leave this field would be no loss,
If only we could get across.

GREAT BIG BILLY [*threateningly*].

There is a bridge across the stream,
But under it two dark eyes gleam.
To cross the bridge I am afraid,
There's something down there in its shade.

BIG BILLY.

There is a bridge across the river,
The thought of crossing makes me shiver,
There is an old, old saying tells
That underneath a monster dwells.

LITTLE BILLY.

What is all this fuss you make?
What makes you two stand there and quake?
I will cross the bridge and see,
Nothing there will frighten me.

GREAT BIG BILLY.

The monster there will eat you quick,
Before you've time to butt or kick.
But you go first and then we'll see
Whether it's also safe for me.

Big Billy.

Although I'm getting thin and thinner,
I don't want to make a dinner
For that creature living there.
I would rather live on air.

Little Billy.

You two big goats stand there and shiver
Because there's something in the river
That neither of you yet has seen.
No wonder you are thin and lean.

Great Big Billy [*longingly*].

That grass across the stream looks fine.
If only some of it were mine!
A juicy meal I badly need
And over there is so much feed.

Big Billy.

I wish I had those apples here,
They are so tempting and so near.
To jump, the river is too wide.
I'm full of emptiness inside.

Little Billy.

I want some fruit and some fresh grass.
The monster will surely let me pass.
I am so small and bony too
I'm sure he will let me go through.

Great Big Billy.

He'll eat you up and that you know.
But if you must take chances, go,
And farewell, little brother mine,
I hope we meet again sometime.

Big Billy.

My little brother, bravely now.
I hope you get across somehow.
And may you safely reach yon fields
Where the ground so richly yields.

LITTLE BILLY.

I am not afraid. He will not eat me.
I am too thin and small you see.
I'm going now, goodbye to you,
And to Great Big Billy too.

[*Exit* LITTLE BILLY. *The others wave, nod at each other and go off.*]

PUPPET POSITIONS FOR SCENE II

[*Bridge centre of stage.*]

When LITTLE BILLY *has crossed the bridge the hand that held him can be used for the other two goats in turn. The operator on the left has* BIG BILLY *and* GREAT BIG BILLY *ready for the short interludes, passes them to the right as required and finishes up with* BIG BILLY *and* LITTLE BILLY *for the final chorus.*

SCENE II

MONSTER [*alone, to audience*].

What do you want crowding here ?
I'll eat you if you come too near.
Yes, you, you look a juicy sight,
Come here, and let me have a bite.

Oh ! how empty I do feel,
I want a big and tasty meal.
[*Pointing to a member of the audience and beckoning.*]
Yon ginger-headed lad looks nice.
He would taste fine with lots of spice.

[*Pointing to another.*]
There's one just there I can't quite place,
[*Searching among the audience and beckoning.*]
That rascal with a dirty face,
A tasty morsel he would be.
Just come up here and let me see.

So what ? You are shy ? All right I'll wait
[*in disgust*]
I'm hungry and it's getting late.
But someone soon will come, I think.
[*looks to the right*]
I hear footsteps on the brink.

O look what comes ! a Billy Goat.
Just the food on which I dote.
Oh ! how happy I shall be
When that goat is inside me.

This bridge is mine. No one goes here
Unless I give him passage clear.
I'll hide until he gets right on,
And don't you tell him where I've gone.
[*Admonishing the audience. Goes down.*]

LITTLE BILLY [*singing*].
I am the Little Billy Goat Gruff,
etc.

[*Stops, looks both sides of the bridge.*]
Here is the bridge. It looks all right.
Why did my brothers take such fright ?
There's nothing here that I can see.
I'm sure that it is safe for me.
What do you think ? [*to audience.*]

[*There is opportunity here for a little backchat with the audience—not too much.*]

MONSTER [*appears on the left side of the bridge*].

Over my bridge, trip, trap, I hear
The sound of running feet.
Someone is crossing my bridge, I fear.
Whom now shall we meet?
Who is it comes this way, clip, clap?
Who dares to cross my bridge, trip, trap?

[*Goes over the bridge and meets* LITTLE BILLY *in the middle.*]

LITTLE BILLY

Little Billy Gruff is my name,
The rich field yonder is my aim.
On this side gone is all the food,
But over there it looks so good. [*pointing*]

MONSTER

There's something I would like to say.
[LITTLE BILLY *retreats.*]
I'm hungry too, so here you stay.
And I will eat you up, you see
Two of us need not hungry be.

LITTLE BILLY [*cringing*].

O sir, I'm much too small and thin,
My ribs are sticking through my skin.
If you eat me, then, sir, I fear
Your tummy ache would last a year.
But after me there comes another, [*confidentially*]
Big Billy Goat Gruff, my brother.
He's big and fat. Somehow I feel
That he would make a proper meal.

MONSTER [*feels all round him*].

It's true, there's nothing much on you.
I wait for Billy Goat number two.
Yes, you can pass. Across you go
And meanwhile I will wait below.

[MONSTER *goes down*, LITTLE BILLY *crosses the bridge and goes out.*]

[*Remove bridge.*]

SCENE III

GREAT BIG BILLY.

Big Billy Goat Gruff, just look, just look.
Little Billy Goat Gruff is across the brook.
He is eating all that wonderful stuff,
Just look, Big Billy Goat Gruff.

BIG BILLY.

O what a feast he has up there,
And we stand here, we hungry pair.
We shall famish if we stay.
I wonder how he found the way ?

GREAT BIG BILLY.

A juicy thistle he's eating now,
And now a piece of hawthorn bough.
What's that ? A turnip top he's got,
And we watch while he eats the lot.

BIG BILLY.

Here no longer will I stay.
To yonder fields I find the way.
My inside will no longer wait
Now I go to meet my fate.

[*Goes off. Exit* GREAT BIG BILLY.]

SCENE IV

[*Bridge as before.*]

MONSTER.

I hear footsteps on the brink.
Someone is coming here I think.
It is Big Billy Goat Gruff I see,
He should make a meal for me.

This bridge is mine. No one goes here
Unless I give him passage clear.
I'll hide until he gets right on,
And don't you tell him where I've gone.

[*Admonishing the audience. Goes down.*]

BIG BILLY [*singing*].

I am the Big Billy Goat Gruff,
etc.

Here is the bridge. It looks all right.
I wonder why we took such fright.
There is nothing here that I can see,
I'm sure that it is safe for me.
Do you think so ? [*to audience.*]

[*More backchat.*]

MONSTER [*as before*].

Over my bridge, trip, trap, I hear
The sound of running feet.
Someone is crossing my bridge I fear.
Whom now shall we meet ?
Who is it comes this way, clip, clap ?
Who dares to cross my bridge, trip, trap ?

[*Meeting in the middle.*]

BIG BILLY.

Big Billy Goat Gruff is my name,
The rich field yonder is my aim [*points*].
On this side gone is all the food,
But over there it looks so good.

MONSTER.

There's something I would like to say:
[BIG BILLY *retreats.*]
I'm hungry too, so here you stay.
And I will eat you up. You see
Two of us need not hungry be.

BIG BILLY.

O sir, I am thinner than you think,
See how my flesh begins to shrink.
I am only skin and bones
You might as well eat a bag of stones.

But after me, there comes another, [*confidentially*]
Great Big Billy Goat Gruff, my brother.
He's big and fat. Somehow I feel
That he would make a proper meal.

MONSTER [*poking him in the ribs and elsewhere*].

It's true. You're not as fat as a flea,
I wait for Billy Goat Number Three.
Yes, you can pass. Across you go,
And meanwhile, I will wait below.

[*Goes down.* BIG BILLY GOAT *crosses and goes out.*]

[*Remove bridge.*]

SCENE V

GREAT BIG BILLY.

What is it yonder that I see?
Big Billy Goat Gruff is waving to me.
He must have crossed the bridge all right.
Those two are gorging. What a sight!

I will not stop longer here.
Two have crossed the bridge, that's clear.
If they can cross, I'll do the same
Or Great Big Billy is not my name.

[*Exit.*]

SCENE VI

[*Bridge as before.*]

MONSTER [*as before*].

I hear footsteps on the brink.
Someone is coming here I think.
It is Great Big Billy Goat Gruff I see.
He should make a meal for me.

This bridge is mine. No one goes here
Unless I give him passage clear.
I'll hide until he gets right on
And don't you tell him where I've gone.
[*Goes down.*]

GREAT BIG BILLY [*singing*].
I am the Great Big Billy Goat Gruff,
etc.
Here is the bridge. It looks all right.
I wonder why we took such fright.
There's nothing here that I can see
I'm sure it is quite safe for me.
Do you think so ?
[*Backchat with audience.*]

[*While* GREAT BIG BILLY *is talking with the audience, the* MONSTER *peeps over the bridge, disappearing again when* BILLY *turns in his direction. When* BILLY *turns left the* MONSTER *appears on the right, as if dodging him.* BILLY *asks the audience if they can see the* MONSTER. *As he turns to look the* MONSTER *disappears. When* BILLY *goes down to look for him, he appears above and disappears again as* BILLY *comes up. The audience will help and this can be continued* ad lib. *Finally,* BILLY *tells the audience he is tired of their jokes and he is going to cross.*]

MONSTER [*as before*].
Over my bridge, trip, trap, I hear
The sound of running feet.
Someone is crossing my bridge I fear.
Whom now shall we meet ?
Who is it comes this way, clip, clap ?
Who dares to cross my bridge, trip, trap ?
[*Meeting in the middle.*]

GREAT BIG BILLY.
Great Big Billy Goat Gruff is my name.
The rich field yonder is my aim.

On this side gone is all the food,
But over there it looks so good.

MONSTER.

There's something I would like to say.
I'm hungry too, so here you stay.
And I will eat you up. You see
Two of us need not hungry be.

GREAT BIG BILLY.

What, you will not let me pass this way?
You want to eat me up, you say.
Then come and show yourself, say I.
You wish to eat me. Come and try.

MONSTER.

You blow yourself up like a bull,
But I your silly beard will pull,
[*tries to pull the beard*]
Tie horns and tail in one big knot
And put you in my stewing-pot.
[*They begin to fight, then pause.*]

GREAT BIG BILLY.

You wicked troll, you stand and shout,
But when my head goes down, look out.
And if you only turn a bit
My horns will catch you where you sit.
[*Another round of boxing, then pause.*]

MONSTER.

I'll eat you up. I'll get you yet.
Many a goat before I've met.
I'll swing you round and round and round
And round and round right off the ground.
[*More fighting.* GREAT BIG BILLY *lands a punch which dazes the monster.*]

GREAT BIG BILLY.

You may well stand there and shiver,
For now I'll pitch you in the river.

Eat me, would you ? No, I think
What you need is a good long drink.

[*Butts the* MONSTER *with his horns.* MONSTER *disappears.*]

[*Calling to the others.*]

Brothers Gruff, Brothers Gruff.

ALL. The bridge is free is free is free,
Is free for you and free for me.
Ripe are the berries, green is the grass,
Over the bridge now all can pass.

THE THREE GOATS [*singing, facing the audience.*]
We are the Billy Goats Gruff,
etc.

[*The audience can be invited to join in a repetition of the chorus.*]

[THE THREE GOATS *bow and go out.*]

THE OWL

(*Acting time 20 minutes*)

CHARACTERS

THE OWL	NEIGHBOUR
JACK	BURGOMASTER
FARMER	

THE OWL is one of the funniest of plays. It has five characters and although it can be performed by two operators, an assistant is useful for fixing swords, etc. Properties required are a sword, spear, pitchfork and axe, which can easily be made out of bits of wood and wire. At the appropriate time these can be fixed to the puppets' right hand by an elastic band. The barn door can either be real scenery or imaginary. If real, an archway, set diagonally across the stage, is sufficient.

The fire is imaginary and the scenery, if any, can easily be pulled down. The torch can either be real or imaginary.

The owl makes its first appearance as a proper puppet. When it makes its flight, a piece of rag on a taut piece of elastic can be released, or the puppet can be hung on a wire and drawn across the top of the stage by a piece of thread.

Apart from one change for the owl, the puppets can remain on the same hands throughout the play.

POSITIONS OF PUPPETS.

JACK [*alone, to the audience*].

Hark, you people all, to me.
Here's a play for you to see.
In the country the scene is set
The actors are together met.
A barn is here, full of hay.
There are four people in our play
And one monster. You will see,
How everything depends on me.
On the farm I work, you know,
I plough and plant and reap and mow.
My name is Jack. I also feed
The stock and get them all they need.
But I must get to work I fear,
I see the master's coming here.

[*Goes out.*]

FARMER [*alone, boasting to the audience*].

The fields and trees that you can see,
The stock and crops belong to me.

This farm I own is very fine,
That barn, so full of hay, is mine.
When winter comes with frost and snow
My animals won't starve, you know.
That barn contains all it can hold.
That hay is worth a heap of gold.

[NEIGHBOUR *enters, and claps him on the shoulder.*]

NEIGHBOUR.

Good friend, how happy must thou be
That I should live right next to thee.
Many crops have we seen grow
And many seasons come and go.
We've stood by one another true
In good times, and in bad ones too.
These twenty years we've neighbours been,
And not one quarrel have we seen.
[*They go out together.*]

BURGOMASTER [*alone, to the audience*].

This village is a happy place
With ne'er a discontented face.
I am the Burgomaster here,
Well known and famous far and near.
If you prefer to call me Mayor,
It's just the same. I shall not care.
I rule here with the law's just might,
And what I say is always right. [*Goes out.*]

JACK [*alone.*]

Now that they've had their little say,
We're ready to begin the play. [*Goes out.*]

OWL [*alone*].

Whoooooooo! Not quite. I must appear
To tell you what I'm doing here.
They think that I'm a monster foul.
I'm not, I'm just a little owl. [*Goes out.*]

[JACK *enters.*]

JACK [*alone*].
Work on this farm is never done.
It keeps me always on the run.
The horses have not fed today,
I'll go and fetch some new mown hay.
That will make them glad indeed.
They've worked and they have earned their feed.

[*Goes to the barn door*, R.]

OWL [*screeches*]. Whooooooooooo!

JACK [*terrified and staggering about*].
Oh what, oh what, oh what's in there?
A monster's made himself a lair.
Oh, all you angels rescue me,
The thing is horrible to see.

[*Shouting towards the* L.]

O master, master, quick I pray,
A monster's hiding in your hay
With eyes like saucers and a shout
Which makes my heart turn inside out.

[*Enter* FARMER.]

FARMER [*looking him up and down*].

Now, what's the cause of all this row?
Jack, don't be such a baby now.
You stand and shiver. Your teeth chatter.
Now tell me, boy, what is the matter?

JACK [*stammering*].

There's something there gave me a fright.
I never saw more awful sight.
O sir, a monster's hiding there.
Just look yourself, but do take care.

FARMER.

Now, boy, don't let your courage sink,
A mouse would frighten you, I think.
I'll see of what this monster's made,
There's no need to be afraid.
Just watch a brave man handle this.
I'll soon see if aught's amiss.
[*Goes to the barn door.*]

OWL. Whoooooooooo!

FARMER [*staggering back*].

O help, O help, what can it be ?
O mercy, mercy, I must flee.
Quite right you are this time, my lad,
In there is something black and bad.
Please fetch my neighbour brave and true,
Perhaps he'll know what we should do.
[JACK *goes out and returns with neighbour.*]

NEIGHBOUR [*to* FARMER].

Now, friend, what's all the noise about?
I thought I heard you scream and shout.
[*Examining him.*]
Your breath is short, your face is pale,
Your teeth are chattering. Tell your tale.

Farmer [*stuttering*].

I can't. I've lost my power of speech.
Such a creature. Such a screech.
A monster foul sits in my hay.
He scratched me as I came away.

Neighbour [*in a superior tone*].

Tut—tut. Don't let your courage sink.
A mouse would frighten you, I think.
I'll see of what this monster's made,
There's no need to be afraid.
Just watch a brave man handle this,
I'll soon see if aught's amiss.

[*Goes to the barn door.*]

Owl. Whoooooooooooo!

Neighbour [*falls and shouts*].

O help, O help, alas, alack,
There's something clawing at my back!
What awful noise, what dreadful shout!
Let me get out, let me get out!

[*Gets up.*]

There's something terrible in there.
It tried to seize and tear my hair.
The Burgomaster here we need,
A worthy man in word and deed.

Farmer.

Jack, quickly fetch him here to us.
The monster shall not treat us thus.

[Jack *goes out.*]

In this task he will gladly share
And get the creature out of there.

[*Re-enter* Jack *with* Burgomaster.]

Burgomaster [*to* Farmer *and* Neighbour, *very sedately*].

Good day, sir, and to you, good day.
What is this phantom in the hay?

I hear you're in a sorry plight.
Well, trust to me, I'll put things right.
Just briefly your distress explain,
[*Pats his head.*]
And trust to my all-powerful brain.

JACK. O honoured sir, act quick I pray.
A monster's hiding in that hay
With eyes like saucers and a shout
Which makes my heart turn inside out.

FARMER.
A creature foul sits in my hay,
He scratched me as I ran away.
My senses and my limbs went numb,
I thought that my last hour had come.

NEIGHBOUR.
He's dreadful, of gigantic size,
Like millstones are his two round eyes.
He shrieked and clawed and spit at me
And tore my hair as I did flee.

BURGOMASTER.
You are a weak-knee'd, nervous lot,
Your talk is foolish tommy rot.
You should not let your courage sink,
A mouse would frighten you, I think.
I'll see of what this monster's made,
There's no need to be afraid.
Just watch a brave man handle this.
I'll soon see if aught's amiss.
[*Goes to the barn door.*]

OWL. Whoooooooooooo!

BURGOMASTER [*terrified*].
O woe is me, what dreadful sound!
The earth is shaking underground.
O heavens help, O pity me!
O what a dreadful sight to see!

[*Pulling himself together.*]

O truly, friends, this is a case
To make the strongest turn his face.
But we will oust him from the barn
Before the village comes to harm.
Fetch swords and spears and pitchforks, too,
And stand by one another true.
No monster shall us thus defy,
We'll shift him out if thus we die.

[JACK, FARMER *and* NEIGHBOUR *go out. Re-enter* JACK *with sword.*]

JACK. This sword I'll wield while I have breath
And fight the monster unto death.

[*Re-enter* FARMER *with spear.*]

FARMER.
Forward to attack the foe,
With this spear I'll make him go.

[*Re-enter* NEIGHBOUR *with pitchfork.*]

NEIGHBOUR.
Soon we'll right my neighbour's wrongs.
This pitchfork has two pointed prongs.

ALL. With heart and hand and courage true,
With sword and spear and pitchfork, too,
Forward then to join the fray,
The victory will be ours today.
Onward, on, to meet the foe,
Forward valiantly we go,
Together we, without a doubt,
Will drive the horrid monster out.

BURGOMASTER.
Now, troops, advance. Deploy your might.
Swordsman, outflank him from the right.
Advance from left who bears the spear,
The pitchforker, attack his rear.

[*They take their stations.*]

All. Repeat chorus.

[*They go to the door of the barn.*]

Owl. Whoooooooooooo!

[*They retreat in confusion.*]

Burgomaster.

The dolts, the cowards, helpless flee.
O what a shameful sight to see !
Their courage sinks into their boots
If this creature merely hoots.

Come, friends, you need a leader brave.
Your reputation I will save.

[*Fetches an axe while the others stand shivering.*]

Come follow me and with this axe
I'll deal him a few hefty cracks.

Farmer [*to* **Burgomaster**].

Yes, you go first, we'll follow you

[*Quietly to the others.*]

And keep our distance this time too.

All. Repeat Chorus.

[**Burgomaster** *leads them to the door and enters. The others stay outside.*]

Owl. Whooooooooooooo!

Burgomaster [*shrieking and speaking off-stage*].

O murder, help, a fire wind blows,
The smell of brimstone's in my nose!
Let me get out, O let me flee,
He's tearing pieces out of me!

[*Comes flying back on to the stage.*]

This task is not so lightly done.
The battle has not yet been won.
The monster did not even shrink,
Let's rest awhile that I may think.

NEIGHBOUR.

Your honour is a clever man.
We know that you will find a plan.

[*Dead silence.*]

BURGOMASTER [*suddenly*].

No use it is our strength bewail,
But cunning works where strength might fail.
On fire the barn and hay we'll set
And so destroy the monster yet.

FARMER [*indignantly*].

Eh ! what ! You'd burn my barn, my hay,
But these are mine. O nay, nay, nay.

BURGOMASTER.

Of no one but yourself you think.
Your selfishness begins to stink.
Destroyed this creature there must be.
If your barn burns, then willingly
You should agree to see it fall.
'Tis for the welfare of us all.

FARMER [*humbly*].

Your worship is a worthy man
Whose brain thinks quicker than mine can.
One cannot but your words admire,
Go, quickly, Jack, and bring some fire.

[JACK *goes out.*]

NEIGHBOUR.

His honour is a clever man
To think of such a mighty plan.
The monster there will soon be dead
And we can safely go to bed.

[JACK *returns with a torch and gives it to the* BURGOMASTER *who throws it into the barn.*]

[FIRE, *and* OWL *flies away over the top of the stage* :]

Whoooooooooooo!

BURGOMASTER [*looking up*].
O what was that flew swiftly by
Out and up into the sky?

FARMER.
It was an owl, an owl, an owl,
An owl it was, no monster foul,
And now my barn is burning down [*angry.*]
You, Burgomaster, you're a clown.

BURGOMASTER [*indignantly*].
Who sent for me with dithering knees ?
Who was first frightened? Tell me please.

FARMER [*getting more and more angry*].
Who said that we should burn the barn ?

NEIGHBOUR [*in support*].
Who is the cause of all the harm ?

FARMER.
The Burgomaster is a dolt.

NEIGHBOUR.
Yes, this trouble's all his fault.

FARMER.
An interfering stupid ass.

NEIGHBOUR.
He's brought things to a pretty pass.

FARMER.
Be off, you must have gone insane.

NEIGHBOUR.
Yes, and don't come back again.
[*They throw him out.*]

FARMER.
And you're a neighbour fine indeed.

NEIGHBOUR.
Who sent for me in time of need?

JACK. You should have seen it was an owl.

Farmer.

You should have known it by its howl.

Jack. A fine friend you, good and true.

Farmer.

Get off my ground and quickly too.

[*They throw him out.*]

Farmer [*stamping up and down*].

A fine mess they have made of this.
There's something in their heads amiss.
A pair of crazy, stupid men,
There's no one can compare with them.

[*Suddenly looks at* Jack *and approaches him.*]

And you were in this mix-up too.
There's something I would say to you,
I know who started this affair.

Jack. O master, see those people there,

[*indicating the audience*]

All sitting quietly, row on row,
They've all been watching us, you know.
They sit with open mouths and eyes
And ask themselves if you've been wise.
They know about the owl and you,
Your friend and Burgomaster too.
They're going to laugh at you, you know,
Before they start, come on, let's go.

[*They go out.*]

RUMPELSTILTSKIN

(*Acting time 20 minutes.*)

CHARACTERS

RUMPELSTILTSKIN
KING
MILLER
GIRL, *later* QUEEN
MESSENGER

Another story, always attractive to children, is Rumpelstiltskin. The play is simple to perform. It has five characters. A spinning-wheel is easily made out of a piece of cardboard and can be fixed to a wooden framework. It should be able to turn. A baby's cot is needed. The other things, necklace, ring, straw and gold can be imaginary.

OPENING POSITIONS OF PUPPETS

SCENE I

[KING *and* MILLER *enter.*]

KING. I am a king for all to see,
I rule a country fair and free.

MILLER. I am a miller brave and strong,
The sails of my mill make a merry song.

KING. My kingdom stretches far and wide,
With splendid towns, rich countryside.

MILLER. The sails of my mill go round and round,
And as they turn the grain is ground.

KING. To rule my kingdom I need gold,
And not enough my coffers hold.

MILLER. I need no gold. I need good wheat
That all may have good bread to eat.

KING. Who else lives at the mill with you ?
Have you a wife and children too ?

MILLER. I have a daughter, not only fair,
But she has other gifts quite rare.

KING. What are these gifts of which you speak?

MILLER. Sire, she is shrewd. If gold you seek,
She can spin it out of straw.

KING. I've never heard the like before.
Quickly, bring her here to me.

MILLER. I'll send her to your Majesty.

[*Goes out.*]

KING. Turn straw to gold. Can this be done ?
Can straw to shining gold be spun ?
This girl's powers are rare indeed,
If she can help me in my need
And turn base straw to gold so fine,
Oh, what a fortune will be mine.

[GIRL *enters.*]

GIRL. Your Majesty, I'm here you see.
You were pleased to send for me.

KING. Good child, I've work for you,
Come, I'll show you what to do.

[*They go out. The spinning-wheel should be put on to the stage. They re-enter.*]

SCENE II

KING. Here is straw, the room no more can hold.
By dawn this must be spun to gold.
The door will be locked fast tonight.
I will return when it is light.
Straw to gold, your father said,
Spin it then or lose your head.

[*Goes out.*]

GIRL. The king has locked the door I fear,
And I am all alone in here.
Oh, what a horrid thing he said,
" Turn straw to gold, or lose your head."
Of all the fateful, cruel tasks,
I cannot do the thing he asks.
Alas, this work I cannot do. [*Crying.*]

[RUMPELSTILTSKIN *enters.*]

RUMPELSTILTSKIN.
Sweet girl, good-morrow to you.
You are so sad and seem to cry.
Have no fear, child. Tell me why.

GIRL. Alas, my heart is sad and cold,
For I must turn this straw to gold.
It must be done the king has said,
And if it's not, I'll lose my head.

RUMPELSTILTSKIN.
This is not an easy task.
If I assist, what may I ask ?
For help, what will you give to me ?

GIRL. I do not know, but let me see,
Perhaps this necklace here would do.
If that is pay enough for you.

RUMPELSTILTSKIN [*examines it*].
Agreed. The necklace I will take,
And quickly straw to gold I'll make.

Spin, wheel, spin, [*Spinning the wheel.*]
Thick and thin,
Straw must be
Carefully
Spun to gold.
Now behold.

All was straw
Here before,
Now instead
Gold is spread
On the ground
All around.

Spin, wheel, spin,
Thick and thin,
Straw will be
Carefully
Spun to gold.
'Tis done. Behold!

There is the gold, all fresh and new.
Until we meet again, adieu. [*Disappears.*]

GIRL. Oh, thanks. Goodbye. The work is done.
The gold is shining like the sun.
It sparkles brightly on the floor.
I never saw so much before.
It must be near the break of day.
I wonder what the king will say?

[*The* KING *enters.*]

KING. I see the straw is turned to gold,
And it's true what I was told.
My child, you have worked well indeed,
But not enough. More gold I need.
Come, you shall work again for me.

[*Move across the stage and back again.*]
Here a bigger room with straw you see.
Turn it into gold I say,
Or you will die at break of day.
[*Goes out.*]

GIRL. Oh, what a heap of straw is here,
And heavy is my heart with fear.
What made my father tell the king
That I could do this magic thing?
Again the king has locked the door.
A little man helped me before,
Alone this work I cannot do.
[RUMPELSTILTSKIN *enters.*]

RUMPELSTILTSKIN.
Shall I fulfil this task for you?
Once again I'll help, you see,
But what is my reward to be?

GIRL. I'll gladly give to you my ring.

RUMPELSTILTSKIN.
All right. It's quite a pretty thing.
Spin, wheel, spin
etc. [*Spinning the wheel.*]
More shining gold I've spun for you.
Until we meet again, adieu. [*Disappears.*]

GIRL. Goodbye. Accept my thanks I pray.
Soon will come the dawn of day.
The straw is gold, the task is done,
Every bit to gold is spun.
Ah, what a marvel here I see.
Now the king will set me free.
[*The* KING *enters.*]

KING. I'm pleased to see this task is done,
Yet still you have another one.
A third night you shall spin for me.
When this is done successfully

And only gold in here is seen,
You shall become my bride and queen.

[*They move across the stage and back again.*]

Here is the room. To work I pray.
Quickly comes the break of day.

[*Goes out.*]

GIRL. I thought the king would set me free,
And now another task I see
Far bigger than the other two.
Alone this work I cannot do.
The little man came twice before,
I wonder : will he come once more?

[RUMPELSTILTSKIN *enters.*]

RUMPELSTILTSKIN.
You see, fair maid, I'm here again,
You did not think of me in vain.
If I should do this work my way,
What will you give me this time, pray ?

GIRL. Alas, I know not what to do.
I've nothing left to give to you.

RUMPELSTILTSKIN.
When you are queen, then give to me
Your first-born child. Do you agree ?

GIRL. Oh, yes, but hurry please tonight.
There's much to do before it's light.

RUMPELSTILTSKIN.
Spin, wheel, spin,
etc. [*Spinning the wheel.*]

Three times this task I've done for you,
Until we meet again, adieu. [*Disappears.*]

GIRL. Three times a room of straw I've seen,
Three times the little man has been,
Three times the straw was turned to gold.
The task is done. I can be bold.

The king will come and I shall be
His bride and queen, happy and free.

[*The* KING *enters.*]

This is the finest sight I've seen.
Now come with me and be my queen.

[*They both go out. The spinning-wheel is removed.*]

SCENE III

[*The cot is put on the stage.*]

QUEEN. One year married we have been,
One year have I been the queen.
A little one has come to us,
Rock him in his cradle thus,
Sleep, my pretty little one,
Night is coming, day is done.

[RUMPELSTILTSKIN *enters.*]

RUMPELSTILTSKIN.
Good evening, Queen. You remember me.
I've come for my reward, you see.

QUEEN. My little babe you cannot take,
Another present I will make,
Gold, or silver, or jewels fine.

Rumpelstiltskin.
No, the baby shall be mine.

Queen. You cannot take my babe away.

Rumpelstiltskin.
The child belongs to me, I say.

Queen. Please let me keep my baby dear.

Rumpelstiltskin.
The babe must come with me I fear.

Queen. Oh, leave my baby, sir, be kind,
And something else for you I'll find.
Without my babe I could not live.

Rumpelstiltskin.
Then three days' grace to you I'll give,
If in that time you guess my name,
The babe I will no longer claim. [*Disappears.*]

Queen. Three days he has given me
To find out what his name may be.
What name best fits the little man ?
I'll send to find out all I can.
Ho, messenger, come here to me.

[Messenger *enters.*]

Messenger.
How can I serve your Majesty ?

Queen. My messenger, go search the land,
Enquire of all, in every stand,
What are their names, and bring also
A full report that I may know
The queer, the odd, the strange names all,
This dwarf I'll know then how to call.

Messenger.
As you command, thus will I do,
And quickly find the name for you.

[*Goes out.*]

Queen. Sleep, my pretty little one,
Night is coming, day is done.

[*Goes out to mark passage of time and comes in again.* RUMPELSTILTSKIN *enters.*]

RUMPELSTILTSKIN.
Your Majesty, I'm here again,
Tell me, have you guessed my name?

QUEEN. It's Timothy, or is it Tom,
Reuben then, or perhaps John?

RUMPELSTILTSKIN.
Not one of those belongs to me.

QUEEN. Cuthbert, or Montmorency,
Fitzgerald, William, Obadiah,
Benjamin, or Jeremiah.

RUMPELSTILTSKIN.
No, you must think of yet more names.

QUEEN. Noel, Andrew, George, or James,
Daniel, Matthew, Robert, Sam,
Leo, Francis, Jesse, Ham.

RUMPELSTILTSKIN.
No, Queen, tomorrow I will come again.
You have not mentioned yet my name.
[*Disappears.*]

QUEEN. The little man's already gone.
His name must be a curious one.
I wonder what that name can be?
But night is coming fast, I see.
Sleep, my pretty little one,
Night is coming, day is done.

[*Goes out and comes back.* RUMPELSTILTSKIN *enters.*]

RUMPELSTILTSKIN.
Good morrow, Queen, your guess I pray.
This morning is the second day.

QUEEN. Your name a curious one must be.
I think perhaps it's Longnosy,

Or Crookshanks, Flatfeet, Shortycrop,
Beaverchin, Hunchback, Baldytop.

RUMPELSTILTSKIN.
Not one of those you've said is mine.
[*Chuckles, laughs and gloats.*]
Do you know any more this time ?

QUEEN. Bandylegs, Footlefoot, tell me please,
Could it be Scruffy. or Bonyknees ?

RUMPELSTILTSKIN.
Tomorrow you must guess again,
You have not mentioned yet my name.
[*Disappears.*]

QUEEN. My pretty babe, what shall we do?
I could not live apart from you.
I hope my messenger indeed,
Can find the name we so much need.
It's time that he was back again,
I trust his search was not in vain.

[*Knock is heard.* MESSENGER *enters and bows.*]

MESSENGER.
Your Majesty, the name I've found.
I travelled all your land around,—
In valley deep, amid the trees
I saw a fire bright in the breeze ;
Upon one leg a dwarf danced there
Singing this song without a care :
" Merrily the feast I'll make,
Today I'll brew, tomorrow bake.
Merrily I'll dance and sing,
Tomorrow will a baby bring,
The lady cannot guess my game,
Rumpelstiltskin is my name."

QUEEN. You have done well. My thanks to you.
In gold shall you receive your due,

And honour shall be yours as well.
My gratitude no words can tell.

[*She dismisses* MESSENGER, *who goes out.*]

Sleep, my pretty little one,
Night is coming, day is done.

[*She goes out and comes back.* RUMPELSTILTSKIN *enters.*]

RUMPELSTILTSKIN.
Now, Queen, please guess, this third, last time.
If you guess wrong, the child is mine.

QUEEN. Is it Wynn, or Jim, or Jeremy,
[*With pauses and deliberation.*]
Or might it Rumpelstiltskin be?

RUMPELSTILTSKIN [*angrily*].
Some witch has told my name to you.
It seems I'm robbed of my just due.
[*Jumps up and down.*]
My foot's gone through the floor I fear,
O let me get outside of here.
[*Disappears.*]

QUEEN. He's gone, the name was right, I see,
The baby is now safe with me.
Safely sleep, my pretty one,
Night is coming, day is done.

[*Sings a lullaby.*]

"Golden slumbers kiss your eyes" *or* Brahm's "Cradle Song."

[*Goes out.*]

THE TRAVELLING MUSICIANS.

(*Acting time* 15 *minutes*)

CHARACTERS

DONKEY	CAT
DOG	COCKEREL

ROBBER

The Musicians of Bremen is another popular story, transferred here to Leeds for its scene of action, but any name can be used to give the play local colour. There are four animal characters, donkey, dog, cat, cockerel, and one robber. Narrative is used as a connecting link.

The cockerel can be fixed on a stiff wire so that it is possible to push him up to his perch. The perch is merely a little shelf in the side of the stage framework. A table is required. Food, drink and other properties can be left to the imagination.

The positions for the puppets are fairly constant throughout. When the cockerel has been placed on his perch the left hand of the operator is free to work the robber. Otherwise there is no change.

Voices characteristic of the animals should be used.

SCENE I

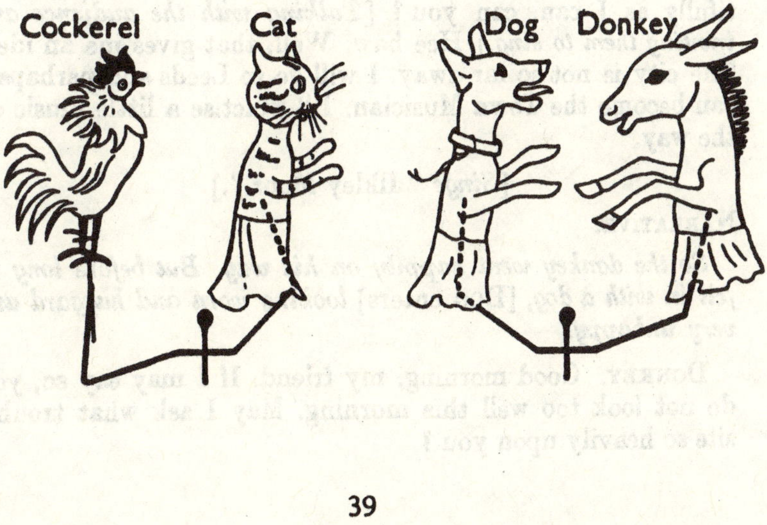

NARRATIVE.

Once upon a time, in the county of Yorkshire, there lived a donkey. [DONKEY enters.] *He was of a kindly nature, hard-working and honest. He had served his master faithfully and well for many a long year. But now he had grown old and could not fulfil his tasks so well. He longed to retire to some quiet corner of a field where he could seek out the juiciest thistles and dream his day dreams. He felt the heaviness of his master's cart and the steepness of the hills more keenly every day and although he did not outwardly rebel, he knew that his master was getting more and more displeased with him. In fact he knew that his master was getting tired of keeping him and was thinking of some way of putting an end to him. That some misfortune would soon overtake him the donkey well knew. He decided, therefore, to take himself off, and one day he jumped over the wall which surrounded his field and went away down the lane, saying to himself:*

DONKEY. No, I will not stay here and meet an untimely end. I will go out into the world and see what I can find. There must be some place for a poor, old tired donkey. At least my voice is still good. Hee haw. [*To audience.*] Pretty, isn't it ? Melodious, isn't it ? Not one of you can sing as beautifully as I can, can you ? [*Talking with the audience and inviting them to sing.*] Hee haw. Well, that gives me an idea. The city is not so far away. I will go to Leeds and perhaps I can become the Town Musician. I'll practise a little music on the way.

[*Sings* " Ilkley Moor ".]

NARRATIVE.

So the donkey went happily on his way. But before long he fell in with a dog, [DOG enters] *looking worn and haggard and very unhappy.*

DONKEY. Good morning, my friend. If I may say so, you do not look too well this morning. May I ask what trouble sits so heavily upon you ?

DOG. Alas, I go in danger of my life. I have grown old and weak in my master's service and now the ungrateful creature is threatening to knock me on the head because I cannot do my work so well. I have served him faithfully and well, and now this is my reward. I am running away from home.

DONKEY. What a sad predicament, my friend! Men are an ungrateful lot. I too, have been disappointed in the same way. Perhaps you had better join me. I am going along to Leeds to become the Town Musician. Come, let us go together, and let us help the journey along with a little music.

[*Sing, facing the audience and pretending to walk.*]

NARRATIVE.

So the donkey and the dog went happily on their way, but before long they met an old cat [CAT enters] *looking full of care and pulling the most sorrowful face.*

[*They stop.*]

DONKEY. Pardon me, lady, but you are looking very down in the mouth. If I can assist you in any way, I am your servant.

CAT. Well may I look sorrowful. Well may I look sad. Sir, my life is in danger. I am no longer young. My sight is not so good as it was, my claws are not so sharp, I cannot run so fast, I cannot jump so far. Instead of chasing rats and mice I prefer to sleep in front of the fire and have my meals served to me; and because I am growing old and cannot serve my mistress as well as I used to do, she threatens to drown me.

DONKEY. What a catastrophe! What a deplorable fate! What an indescribable outrage! Madam, I think you had better join our company. You have a wonderful voice, especially at night. I think we could use your services. Come along with us. We are going to Leeds to form the Town Band. May I ask you to join us and add variety to our concerts?

CAT. I shall be delighted, delighted. Sir, I am honoured beyond my station.

[*Sing, facing the audience as before.*]

NARRATIVE.

So the donkey and the dog and the cat went happily on their way, but before long they passed a farmyard. Standing on the top of the largest heap of manure [COCKEREL enters] *an old cockerel was bawling at the top of his voice:*

DONKEY. Bravo, bravo, Master Chanticleer. What a song, what a melody, what a famous noise ! But do please tell us the cause of your excitement.

COCK. I sing for the last time. This is my farewell song. Tomorrow guests are coming to the house for dinner and I am to be present—in the form of chicken broth.

DONKEY. What painful news, Master Chanticleer ! What a terrible calamity ! That is a fate to be avoided at all costs. Perhaps we could make use of your wonderful voice. Truly, a magnificent instrument. Hark. We are going to Leeds to form the Town Band. Would you care to join our select company ?

COCK. With all my heart, with all my heart.

[*Sing, facing the audience and pretending to walk.*]

NARRATIVE.

So the four friends journeyed on towards the city, but before they arrived night had fallen and they turned aside into a wood to rest themselves until morning.

[*They stop.*]

DONKEY. Well, this is a poor sort of hotel, but I've known worse places. A little hard, perhaps, a little draughty, a little cold. Well, I will make myself as comfortable as I can under this tree and tomorrow maybe I can sleep in the Town Hall.

[*Lies down on the right.*]

DOG. Not much of a place here, even for a dog. Ah, I see the old donkey has lain down. Perhaps if I get close up to him he will keep some of the cold wind off me. Pooh, it's time he had a bath.

[*Lies down on the donkey.*]

CAT. I think this tree will suit me.

[*Lies down centre.*]

COCK. And it's right to the top I'll go for a good perch and a good lookout.

[*Jumps up to a perch.*]

[*Sleep, for a few minutes.*]

COCK [*excitedly*]. Friends, I see something bright and shining at no great distance.

DONKEY [*cross*]. It's the moon. Be quiet.

COCK. Friends, I see something bright and shining at no great distance.

DOG [*cross*]. Stop squawking and be quiet.

COCK. Friends, I see something bright and shining at no great distance.

CAT [*cross*]. I'll pull the feathers from your tail if you wake me again.

COCK. Friends, I see something bright and shining at no great distance. I think it is a light and a house.

[*The animals bestir themselves.*]

DONKEY. In that case, maybe we had better try to change our quarters, for this is not the best lodging in the world and I am hungry. I was dreaming of a nice juicy thistle.

DOG. And I could do with a bone or two.

CAT. A saucer of milk would be wonderfully acceptable.

COCK. I'm quite empty, I'm quite empty.

DONKEY. Let us go towards this light and see what we can find. Softly now. Yes, a house. Not so much noise there. Here's a window. Let me peep.

[*They line up behind the donkey who faces* R.]

COCK. Well, donkey, what can you see ?

DONKEY. I see a table spread with all kinds of good things

and robbers sitting around it about to start their supper.

DOG. I could do with something to eat.

CAT. And me. I've had nothing since yesterday.

COCK. And I'm peckish too.

DONKEY [*turning to the others*]. Listen, comrades. This is our opportunity. This is our chance to show what fine musicians we are. Let us give them a grand concert. Then, maybe they will invite us to join in the feast. At least, they will throw something out to us. Come, I will prop myself on the window-sill. Do you, Squire Dog, climb upon my shoulders. Mistress Cat, will you climb one higher and Master Chanticleer shall perch himself at the top. [*They climb up.*] I will now count three and we will launch forth into song together—One, two three !

[*All sing a different song in their own manner, at the end of which they crash and disappear.*]

NARRATIVE.

But the donkey slipped and with a terrible and hideous crashing and clattering the animals tumbled through the window into the room where the robbers were holding their feast. The robbers thought that some terrible fate had overtaken them and, frightened out of their wits, they rushed away as fast as their legs could carry them.

SCENE II

[*The table should be put into position*, C.]

DONKEY. It's very kind of them to leave us this splendid meal. I think I can do justice to it. Excellent! Magnificent!

[*Helping themselves.*]

DOG. What a wonderful piece of beef this! Not since I was a puppy have I tasted anything so fine.

CAT. May I trouble you for the sauce ?

COCK. What a wonderful repast, to be sure ! I'm nearly making a pig of myself.

DONKEY. Mistress, would you have the goodness to pass me the salt ?

DOG. Master Chanticleer, you must sample this steak and kidney pie.

CAT. What delicious cream this is ! A most satisfying and refreshing meal, I say.

COCK. Mighty fine, mighty fine.

DONKEY. I don't ever recall having enjoyed such a meal before, and, you know, we donkeys live for ever.

DOG. My friend, you are a genius.

CAT. I'm so glad you invited me to come along with you.

COCK. Very satisfactory, very satisfactory.

DONKEY. Ladies and gentlemen, your health!

[*Passes the bottle round—Mime.*]

DONKEY. Ladies and gentlemen, the hour is late. I suggest that each of us retires until the morning. Let each one find the resting place most suited to his nature. For myself, I see a heap of straw in the yard which will make me an excellent couch. I bid you goodnight. [*Lies down* R.]

[*The table is taken away.*]

DOG. This mat by the door will suit me very well. This makes me feel quite at home. Sweet dreams ! [*Lies down right of* C.]

CAT. There's no place like the fire for me. I will curl up on the hearth to rest. [*Lies down* C.]

COCK. I need a perch. I think I'll try the rafters. Here we go. Good night. Good night. [*Goes up on his perch.*]

[*Silence except for snores.*]

NARRATIVE.

So the animals slept in the robbers' house and everything was quiet and at peace. But about midnight, one of the robbers, being somewhat braver than his companions, came back to see if he could find out what had disturbed them. [ROBBER enters left.] *He found the house dark and quiet and crept silently in. The cat half opened her eyes and the robber, thinking that they were glowing coals, took a poker to try to stir them up.* [Pokes at the CAT.]

[*The* CAT *goes for him.*]

CAT. Meeoww, ow, ow.

ROBBER. Oh, a witch, a witch, a witch.

[*The* DOG *goes for him.*]

DOG. Bow, wow.

ROBBER. Oh, a ruffian with a knife.

[*The* DONKEY *goes for him.*]

DONKEY. Hee haw.

ROBBER. Help, a monster with a club!

COCK [*shouting*]. Cock-a-doodle-doo!

[*There is a great deal of noise and commotion.*]

ROBBER. What, the devil himself! Let me get out. O help! O mercy, blood, fire and thunder, let me get out! I'll never come back here again. [*Goes out. The animals lie down again.*]

NARRATIVE.

The robber went back to his friends and told them a terrible story: how a witch had attacked him, and dug her nails into him, and he showed them where the cat had scratched him; how a ruffian had attacked him with a knife, and he showed them where the dog had sunk his teeth into his leg; how a monster with a club had beaten him, and he showed them where the donkey had kicked him; how the devil himself had cried, "Throw the old rascal up here." The robbers were so terrified that they never went back to the house.

But the animals spent the rest of the night in peace and quiet, and when morning came they found themselves in possession of the house. [Animals wake and get up.] *They decided to stay there, and they all lived happily ever after.*

[*Sing and dance.*]

" Half a pound of tuppenny rice " or " Here we go round the Mulberry Bush " or something similar.

[*They bow and go out.*]

THE DRAGON AND THE BOY WITH THE FLUTE

(*Actirg time* 15 *minutes*)

CHARACTERS

FIRST KNIGHT
SECOND KNIGHT
BOY
HERALD
PRINCESS
KING
DRAGON
PEOPLE (*Any number*)

One might call this "The Dragon's Redemption"—a good story with a good ending. There are six characters, the dragon and several unspecified "persons." A piece of cloth for the Princess's scarf can be real or imaginary. The boy's flute can be a piece of rolled cardboard attached to his right hand. There should be a recorder off-stage to produce the music when required.

PUPPET POSITIONS FOR SCENE I

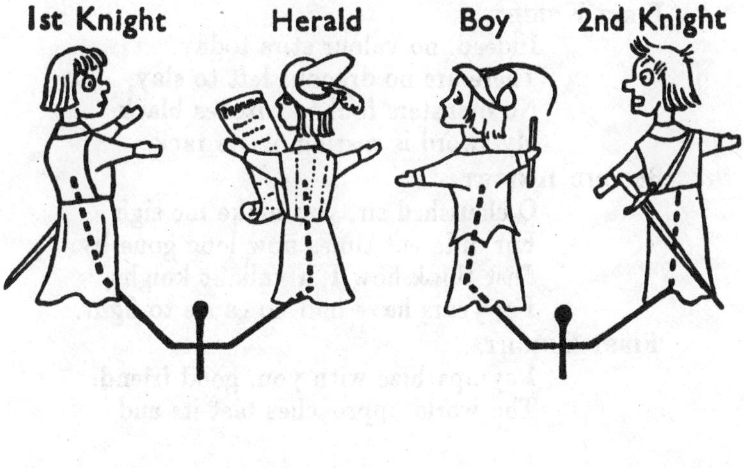

Scene I

[*The* Two Knights *enter.*]

First Knight.

Good day, my friend, how do you do ?
I trust that things are well with you.
Your cheeks are red, your eyes are clear,
Right glad am I to meet you here.

Second Knight.

Sir, my health is good indeed ;
I lack for nothing that I need.
But you, sir, do I see you well ?
Your news to me, my friend, pray tell.

First Knight.

My health is good, my temper fine.
Good food and drink are always mine.
There is but one thing puts me out,
It is too quiet here about.

Second Knight.

O true, my friend, how true you speak.
For knights like us the view is bleak.
No longer dragons roam the earth,
No longer monsters test one's worth.

First Knight.

Indeed, no valour stirs today.
There are no dragons left to slay,
No monsters foul or witches black.
My sword is rusting on its rack.

Second Knight.

O cherished sir, you make me sigh
For different times now long gone by.
Just think how I, a valiant knight,
For years have had no cause to fight.

First Knight.

I sympathize with you, good friend.
The world approaches fast its end

When knights like us have naught to do.
I need some quests and combats new.

SECOND KNIGHT.
The world is dull and still today.
No more adventures come my way.

[*The* BOY *enters.*]

FIRST KNIGHT.
When I was young and in my prime,
I proved my valour many a time.

SECOND KNIGHT.
When I was in the flush of youth,
I did some mighty deeds forsooth.

BOY. O, sirs, your stories should be told.
You must be brave and strong and bold,
With dragons, monsters, fiends to fight.
Please tell me of your deeds of might.

[*The* BOY *stands between the* TWO KNIGHTS *and turns first to one, then the other, during the following dialogue.*]

FIRST KNIGHT.
A horrid dragon I did slay,
Whose breath put out the light of day.

SECOND KNIGHT.
With a monster once I fought a fight
All day long and half the night.

FIRST KNIGHT.
The dragon roared with thunder sound.

SECOND KNIGHT.
The monster's footsteps shook the ground.

FIRST KNIGHT.
He snorted with his fiery breath.

SECOND KNIGHT.
Ah me, I thought, a fight to death.

FIRST KNIGHT.
He looked at me with wicked eye.

SECOND KNIGHT.
I thought, I conquer now or die.

FIRST KNIGHT.
He rushed at me with outspread wing.

SECOND KNIGHT.
We chased each other in a ring.

FIRST KNIGHT.
By now the air with smoke was black.

SECOND KNIGHT.
I jumped and landed on his back.

FIRST KNIGHT.
Underneath his wing I hid.

SECOND KNIGHT.
Behind him then I quickly slid.

FIRST KNIGHT.
His wing beat made a roaring gale.

SECOND KNIGHT.
With both my hands I seized his tail.

FIRST KNIGHT.
His wings together then I bound.

SECOND KNIGHT.
I swung him round and round and round.

FIRST KNIGHT.
Down his throat his tail I threw.

SECOND KNIGHT.
And spinning through the air he flew.

FIRST KNIGHT.
And choked him thus immediately.

SECOND KNIGHT.
Ten miles away he hit the sea.

BOY. O thank you, sirs. Your stories bold
Have almost made my blood run cold.
What strong and brave men you must be
To battle thus courageously!

[HERALD *enters.*]

HERALD. Harken, people, all I pray.
List to what I have to say.
A proclamation here I bring
From your right and lawful king.

A fiery dragon roams the land
Spreading ruin on every hand.
A champion brave and true we seek
To tame or slay the monster quick.
Who rules the beast shall win great fame,
Titles and an honoured name.
His bride shall be the princess fair
And half the kingdom be his share.
Sir knights, you both look strong and brave.
To you we look the realm to save.
You look so valiant, true and bold.

FIRST KNIGHT.
Excuse me, sir, I have a cold,
My chest is weak, my breath is short,
It is high time my bed I sought.

[*He goes out.*]

SECOND KNIGHT.
Sir, my sorrow is sincere.
I cannot fight this time I fear.
I have, although I look so hale,
An awkward, ingrowing toe-nail.

[*He goes out.*]

HERALD. What loud-mouthed braggarts, low born slaves,
What faithless, churlish, scurvy knaves.
Vainglorious dolts with fancy airs,
What empty boasts, what shame is theirs !

BOY. Sir, I will seek this dragon out.
I'm not afraid, you need not doubt.
Here I have my flute, you see,
Which I will take along with me.

Herald. With flute you cannot fight, my boy.
You need a weapon, not a toy.
Are any champions sitting here,
Strong and bold, who know no fear?

[*To the audience.*]

If so, then just come up to me.
There must be some. Who's that I see?
That red nosed fellow sitting there [*pointing*],
Or that one with the ginger hair.
The third one looks a brawny youth.
His face is dirty but in truth,
It might even frighten the dragon away.
Do you feel equal to the fray?

Boy. To tame the dragon I will try,
And either I shall win or die.

Herald. Too young you are, my boy, I trow,
To face this fearsome monster now.
Though brave you are, I cannot see
How you can hope for victory.

Boy. If I can speak nice words to him,
Perhaps he won't be fierce and grim.
A tune upon my flute I'll play
And talk in the politest way.

Herald. You speak so bravely, go, my son.
With courage, victory may be won.
As mascot in your great intent
The young princess's scarf is lent.
May fortune smile upon you, boy,
Success be yours, and every joy.

[**Interval** *during which people appear and disappear, chased by the dragon.*]

The dragon can be centre-stage. A figure pops up on the R. *and disappears as the dragon approaches. Immediately a second figure comes up on the* L.*, the dragon dashes towards it and the action repeats. The dragon can also disappear while the characters* *ask the audience if they have seen him. They pop up and down alternately*, ad lib.

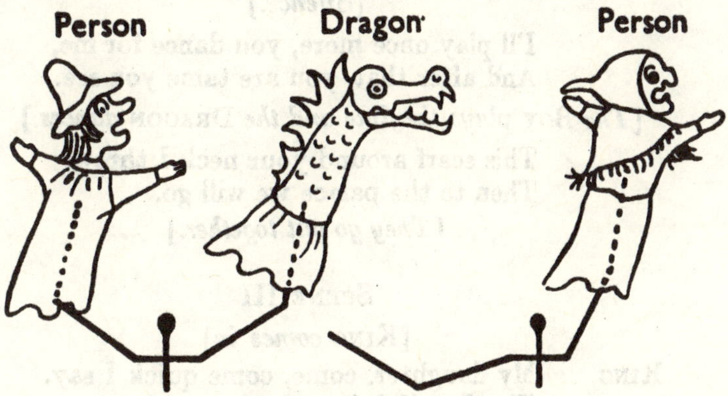

[*They all go out.*]

SCENE II

[*The* DRAGON *settles himself in the* L. *corner. The* BOY *enters.*]

BOY. Ah, there he is, he will see me soon.
Meanwhile, I'll play a little tune.
[*The* DRAGON *roars. The* BOY *plays.*]
Good dragon, nice dragon, down I say.
Another little tune I'll play.
[*The* DRAGON *roars. The* BOY *plays.*]
Please don't bellow any more,
I don't like you when you roar.
[*A mild roar.*]
Please no more breathing fire and flame.
I want you to be nice and tame.
[*A snort.*]
Be quiet now as you've been told.
You see now, he's as good as gold. [*To audience.*]
[*Roars again.*]

How rude you are, and naughty too,
And all these children watching you!

[*Silence.*]

I'll play once more, you dance for me,
And after that, you are tame you see.

[*The* Boy *plays the flute and the* Dragon *dances.*]

This scarf around your neck I throw,
Then to the palace we will go.

[*They go out together.*]

Scene III

[King *comes in*]

King. My daughter, come, come quick I say.
The dreadful dragon comes this way,
Before he strikes his deadly blow,
Run, save yourself, away now, go.

[Princess *enters.*]

Princess.
He does not look so fierce to me
In fact, he walks quite quietly.

He breathes out neither fire nor flame,
But calmly goes and seems quite tame.
A boy is walking by his side.
There seems no need for me to hide.
They are coming closer, getting near—
O father, they are coming here.

KING. What is this wonder that I see?
The dragon seems quite tame to me.
My daughter's scarf is on his head,
And thus quite gently he is led.

[BOY *and* DRAGON *come in.*]

He licks my hand, and seems to bow.
My boy, will you explain this now ?

BOY. Sir, here the dragon I present.
No longer has he ill intent.
His evil ways he's left behind.
He is quite friendly to mankind.

KING. What marvel this, what wonder here !
What miracle doth now appear !
Redeemed the dragon is and freed
From curses by this noble deed.
With steadfast courage it was done.
This is a mighty battle, won
Without a sword, without a spear.
All honour to our champion dear.
This is a memorable day.
Three cheers, you crowd, hip, hip, hooray.

[*To audience.*]

The dragon is a friendly beast.
Then now prepare the marriage feast.
Proclaim the news both far and near,
This boy will wed our princess dear.
Let bells ring out now everywhere
In greeting to the happy pair.
The dragon stays in the palace yard
And joins our faithful, honoured guard.

THE DONKEY, THE TABLE AND THE STICK.

(Acting time 40 minutes)

This play has endless fun in it. It is longer and appears to be a little more complicated than the others. In actual fact it is quite simple once the sequence of events has been grasped. It is a play where the audience has many opportunities of joining in and these should be used to advantage.

There are nine characters and an assistant to the two operators is useful. Properties required are a stick, a table and a cover. The latter can be made out of a cardboard lid with several articles stuck to it. It is slipped over the table from the back at the appropriate moment. The actual eating is done in mime. The shower of gold and silver can be made by attaching small discs of cardboard by thread to the end of a stick, which is manœuvred by one of the operators. In the same hand a tin with a few beads in it can be shaken to produce a sound effect.

CHARACTERS

JACK — **OLD WOMAN** — **CARPENTER**

JILL — **JACK'S FATHER** — **DONKEY**

DWARF — **INNKEEPER** — **TRAVELLER**

OPENING POSITIONS OF PUPPETS

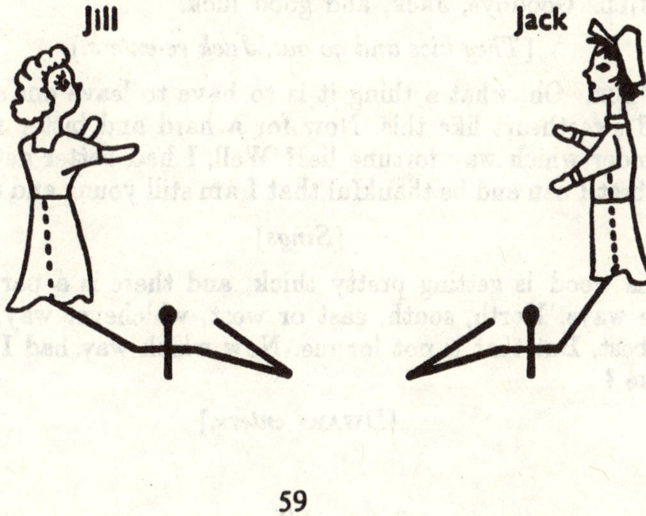

NARRATIVE [JACK *appears alone.*]

Once upon a time there was a Yorkshire lad called JACK. *His father was so cruel that* JACK *decided to leave home and seek his fortune elsewhere. But first he wanted to say goodbye to his sweetheart,* JILL.

JACK. Jill, I am running away from home.

JILL. Why, Jack, what has happened ?

JACK. My father is so nasty and so cruel to me that I will not stay here any longer. He says I may not marry you until I have made my fortune. I am therefore going out into the world to seek it.

JILL. But you will come back to me, Jack ?

JACK. Yes, I shall come back. I will come back when I am rich. Then you and I will become man and wife.

JILL. Oh, Jack, and how long will that be ?

JACK. That I cannot say, but I hope that it will not be too long, and I will always think of you.

JILL. And I will think of you too and wait here for you.

JACK. Goodbye, Jill.

JILL. Goodbye, Jack, and good luck.

[*They kiss and go out. Jack re-enters.*]

JACK. Oh, what a thing it is to have to leave one's home and sweetheart like this. Now for a hard and bitter road. I wonder which way fortune lies? Well, I had better get along as best I can and be thankful that I am still young and strong.

[*Sings*]

This wood is getting pretty thick, and there is a parting of the ways. North, south, east or west, whichever way, home is best. But that is not for me. Now which way had I better take ?

[DWARF *enters.*]

Dwarf. Good morning, Jack.
Jack. Eh, who is there ?
Dwarf. A friend of yours.
Jack. But I have never seen you before.
Dwarf. But I have seen you.
Jack. How did you know my name ?
Dwarf. I am your friend.
Jack. Where did you come from?
Dwarf. Down there.
Jack. Why do you point that way ?
Dwarf. That is your way.
Jack. But, how . . . why . . .
Dwarf. I am your friend.
Jack. Thanks, but . . .
Dwarf. Goodbye, Jack, you deserve good luck.

Jack. The little man has disappeared. That is the way he pointed. All right, I will go along that way and see what happens.

[*Sings.*]

[Old Woman *enters.*]

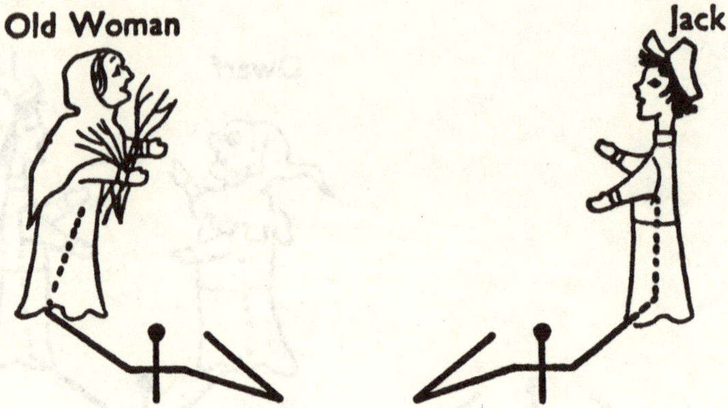

Jack [*to himself*]. Now who is here? An old woman gathering sticks. [*To her.*] Good morning, lady. Can I help you?

Woman. Thank you, young man. I am getting old and I am tired. My back aches and I want some sticks for my fire.

Jack. Let me help you to collect some. [*Collects sticks and gives them to her—mime.*] There, and there and there.

Woman. You are a kind boy. What is your name?

Jack. My name is Jack.

Woman. Well, Jack, you seem a likely lad. Will you stay with me and be my servant?

Jack. Oh, that I will indeed, ma'am.

Woman. Can you sweep, and clean, and cook, and scrub, and make the fires, and chop the wood, and milk the goat and feed the hens?

Jack [*nodding*]. Oh, yes, indeed I can.

Woman. Then you shall live in my house and serve me for a year and a day. Come along with me.

[*They go out together.*]

Narrative.

So Jack took service with the old woman. He served her well for a year and a day and soon his time was up.

[JACK *and the* OLD WOMAN *enter.*]

WOMAN. Jack, I am very pleased with your work.

JACK. I am very pleased to hear it, ma'am.

WOMAN. You have been a good boy, Jack. You have worked well. You have done everything as I have wanted it done.

JACK. I am very glad to have pleased you, ma'am, and to have served you.

WOMAN. Now you shall have your reward. I will give you your wages.

JACK. Oh, thank you, ma'am.

WOMAN. Go to the stable and bring out the first animal you see.

JACK. Yes, ma'am, I will go straightway. [*He goes out.*]

WOMAN. Now he is going to get a surprise. [*He comes back with a donkey.*] You have brought the donkey, have you? That is right. He is yours. That is your wages.

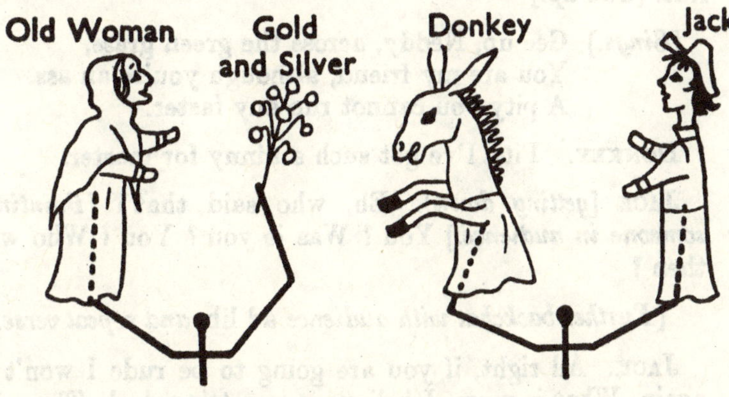

JACK. Thank you, ma'am. It is a lovely gift. I am very pleased with it. Just think, a donkey of my very own!

WOMAN. Ah! but listen, Jack. This is not an ordinary donkey. I will tell you a secret. This is a magic donkey. You have only to pull his ears to make him hee-haw. And every time you pull his ears gold pieces and half-crowns will fall from his mouth.

JACK. Oh, thank you again, ma'am. This is a fine donkey. He looks so kind too, and clever. Come, Neddy, let us be going. Now I have my fortune and I will hurry back to Jill, my sweetheart. Goodbye, ma'am.

WOMAN. Goodbye, Jack, and good luck.

[*Goes out.*]

JACK. Oh, what a fine thing to own a donkey, a fine donkey like this. Every time I pull his ears I get pieces of gold and silver. [*To audience.*] Would you like to see me get some gold and silver ? Watch then. [*Pulls donkey's ears, donkey brays and gives a shower of gold and silver.*] There we are. Well, as you are such nice people I will leave those for you. Come along, Neddy. We will be on our way. I might even try to ride. [*Gets up.*]

[*Sings.*] Gee up, Neddy, across the green grass,
You are my friend, although you're an ass.
A pity you cannot run any faster.

DONKEY. Pity I've got such a ninny for master.

JACK [*getting down*]. Eh, who said that ? [*Pointing to someone in audience.*] You ? Was it you ? You ? Who was it then ?

[*Further backchat with audience* ad lib. *and repeat verse.*]

JACK. All right, if you are going to be rude I won't sing again. What is more, I believe it is getting dark. There is an inn here, I see. I had better stay here for the night and ride home in the morning. Hi, landlord. Hi, innkeeper, hi, you are wanted.

[INNKEEPER *enters.*]

INNKEEPER. Is it you making all the noise ?

JACK. Yes. I want some supper and a bed. Let it be a fine supper and a fine bed. Let it be the finest supper you have ever served, roast pork, green peas and apple sauce, plum pudding and the best wine your cellar holds. [*To audience.*] Have you any suggestions for a good feast ? [*Backchat* ad lib.]

INNKEEPER. This is a fine order, young man, but these things cost money. Show me yours.

JACK. You need not worry about that, my friend. I have plenty of it. Just excuse me for a moment, please. Come this side, Neddy.

[*Pulls the donkey's ears and a shower of gold and silver falls from his mouth.*]

INNKEEPER [*aside*]. What is he doing ? Pulling the donkey's ears. What ! Gold and silver. This donkey must be mine.

[JACK *collects the money and gives it to the* INNKEEPER.]

JACK. There you are, landlord, now serve the best.

INNKEEPER. Certainly, sir, please come this way. I will get you anything you wish. The animal will be quite all right there, sir. Yes, sir, just come this way.

JACK. A feast now, landlord, and then a comfortable bed. Tomorrow I go home to my sweetheart Jill and wedding bells.

[*They go out, leaving the donkey.*]

Narrative.

So Jack was served with an excellent meal and went off to bed to sleep soundly after all his adventures, but meanwhile . . .

[Innkeeper *enters.*]

Innkeeper. Ah, there is the donkey. Well, Jack is safe asleep, and this donkey shall be mine. I have a donkey which looks exactly like this one and if I exchange them, Jack will never notice. Ha, ha, ha, and the magic one I will keep for myself. I will take this [*goes out with the donkey*] and put this *coming back again*] in its place. Ha, ha, ha.

[*N.B.—The same donkey serves the purpose.*]

[*He goes out.*]

Narrative.

So the wicked innkeeper exchanged donkeys and in the morning Jack did not notice what had happened and went towards home feeling very happy and gay.

[*Enter* Jack.]

Jack. Now, Neddy, it is home for us, to meet my Jill and show my father what a fortune I have.

[*Sings on the journey.*]

Here we are at last, and here is my father to meet us.

[*Enter* Father.]

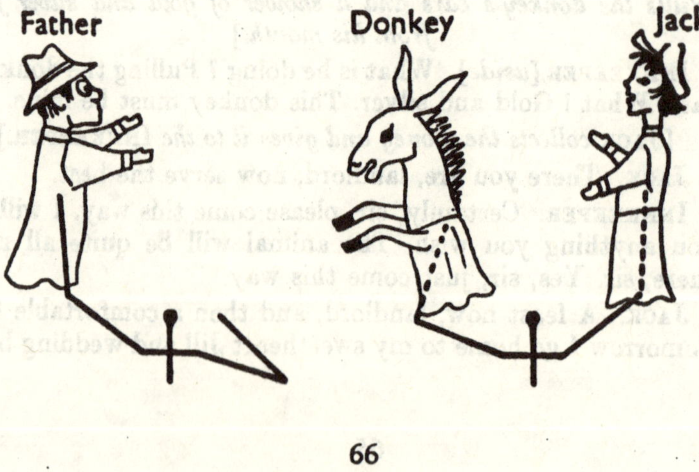

Father. You are soon back.

Jack. Yes, father, and I have my fortune and I intend to marry Jill.

Father. You have your fortune, you say. Then show it to me.

Jack. This donkey is my fortune, father.

Father [*laughing*]. A donkey. It looks to me as if two donkeys have come home.

Jack. But you do not understand. This is not an ordinary donkey. This is a magic donkey. [*To audience*] Isn't it ? I will show you more gold and silver in the next five minutes than you have ever seen before in your life. All I have to do is to pull the donkey's ears.

[*He pulls, the donkey brays, but nothing happens.*]

All I have to do is to pull the donkey's ears.

[*Repeats with some consternation.*]

All I have to do is to pull the donkey's ears.

[*The donkey brays and kicks him.*]

Father. What! You make a laughing stock of me! You lazy, idle, good-for-nothing little scallywag. I'll teach you to play tricks on me. I'll show you.

[*Beats him.* Jack *runs away followed by his* Father.]

[Jack *enters.*]

Jack [*alone*]. What a sorry homecoming to be sure! I thought I had my fortune and my Jill, and all I have are knocks and bruises.

[Dwarf *enters.*]

Position of Puppets as on page 61

Dwarf. Good morning, Jack.

Jack. Oh, you again.

Dwarf. You have lost your donkey, Jack.

Jack. Yes, how did you know ?

Dwarf. I know all about you.

JACK. Then tell me what to do now.

DWARF. Go that way, Jack.

JACK. Why should I go that way?

DWARF. That is your way, Jack.

JACK. What shall I find there?

DWARF. You will see. Be more careful this time.

JACK. How——

DWARF. Goodbye, Jack, and good luck.

[DWARF *disappears.*]

JACK. This way, the little man said. Well, I will go along and see where it leads. [*Sings.*] Here is a workman, and, if I am not mistaken, a carpenter.

[CARPENTER *enters.*]

CARPENTER. Well, my lad, why do you stand gaping there? A strong young man like you should be at work.

JACK. O sir, I am always glad to do some work and to help anyone that I can.

CARPENTER. You seem a likely lad. Will you be my assistant?

JACK. Certainly I will, sir.

CARPENTER. Then you shall live with me and serve me for a year and a day.

JACK. Yes, sir, that I will do gladly.

[*They go out together.*]

NARRATIVE.

So Jack took service with the carpenter and served him well for a year and a day. Whenever he had work to do he did it well and never begrudged a little extra time to do it really well. Soon the time was up.

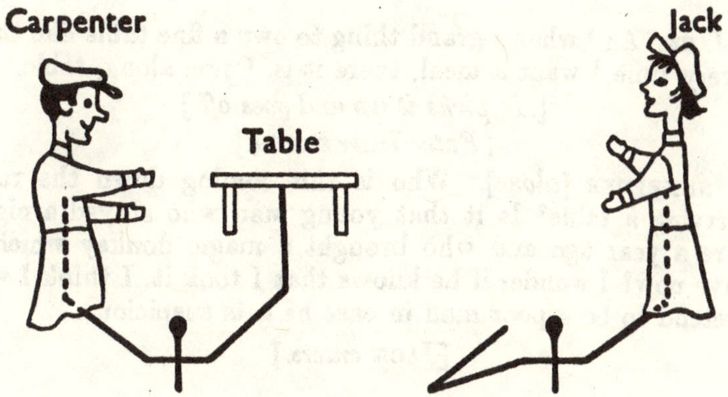

[CARPENTER *and* JACK *enter.*]

CARPENTER. Jack, I am very pleased with your work.

JACK. I am very glad to hear it, sir.

CARPENTER. You have been a good boy, Jack. You have worked well and done everything as I have told you.

JACK. I am very glad to please you, sir, and serve you.

CARPENTER. Now you shall have your reward. I will give you your wages.

JACK. Oh, thank you, sir.

CARPENTER [*bringing a table*]. Here is a table. This is yours. It is your wages.

JACK. Oh, thank you, sir. It is a lovely table. Jill will sit one side and I shall sit the other. I am very pleased to have a table of my own.

CARPENTER. But listen, Jack. I will tell you a secret. This is not an ordinary table. This is a magic table. You have only to say to it, "Table, be covered," and at once it will be weighed down with good things to eat and drink.

JACK. Thank you, thank you. This is a fine table. Now I have my fortune again, I will hurry back to Jill, my sweetheart. Goodbye, sir.

CARPENTER. Goodbye, Jack, and good luck.

[CARPENTER *goes out.*]

Jack. Ah ! what a grand thing to own a fine table like this. Every time I want a meal, there it is. Come along, table.

[*He picks it up and goes off.*]

[*Enter* Innkeeper.]

Innkeeper [*alone*]. Who is this coming down the road carrying a table? Is it that young man who stayed a night here a year ago and who brought a magic donkey which I have now? I wonder if he knows that I took it. I think I will pretend to be a poor man in case he gets suspicious.

[Jack *enters.*]

Jack. Come, landlord. I would like to stay the night with you again. Set meat and drink before me and prepare for me a comfortable bed.

Innkeeper. Alas, sir, I am sorry. My house is not so well visited as it once was and I am now but a poor man. I think I can offer you bread and ale, and perhaps an egg.

Jack. That is poor fare indeed. Why, I can do better than that myself. Just watch. " Table, be covered." [*The table is spread with a feast.*] Do you see what I mean? Well, you see, here is a splendid feast, sufficient for both of us. If you are hungry you had better join me.

Innkeeper. Indeed the sight of such a feast would make anyone hungry. What a spread !

[*They eat and drink.*]

Jack. That is enough for me, I think. I will go to bed. Tomorrow I go home to my sweetheart Jill and wedding bells.

[*He goes out.*]

Innkeeper. Yes, you go to bed, and sleep soundly. And, meanwhile, I think I could make good use of this table. Ha, ha, I will take it away and put another in its place. What do you say ? Jack will not notice the difference, and then this magic table will be mine.

[*He goes off with the table then puts it back again. The same table serves the purpose.*]

Narrative.

So the wicked innkeeper exchanged tables and in the morning Jack did not notice what had happened, and went towards home feeling very happy and gay.

[**Jack** *enters, picks up table and sets off.*]

Jack. Well, table, it's home for you and me. Come along.

[*Sings.*]

Here we are, home again, and my father to meet us.

[**Father** *enters.*]

Father. So you are back again.

Jack. Yes, and I have my fortune with me, and now I intend to marry Jill.

Father. You have your fortune, have you? I hope it is a better one than the last you brought here. Show it to me.

Jack. This table is my fortune, father.

Father. A table. What stuff and nonsense is this !

Jack. But this is a magic table. Isn't it ? [*Turning to the audience.*] I have only to say certain words and the table will be weighed down with the most wonderful things to eat and drink.

Father. Good, then I will join you in the feast.

Jack. All I have to do is to say, "Table, be covered."

[*Nothing happens.*]

All I have to do is to say, "Table, be covered."

[*Consternation.*]

All I have to do is to say——

Father. What, how dare you show yourself here again with this tomfoolery! How dare you make a laughing stock of me! I will show you how to treat me, you rapscallion, you vagabond, you. [*Beats him and drives him off.*]

[Father *goes out and* Jack *enters.*]

Jack [*alone*]. Here I am again, homeless again, and this time I did think that I would have fared better.

[Dwarf *enters.*]

Positions of Puppets as on page 61

Dwarf. Good morning, Jack.

Jack. You again.

Dwarf. You are in trouble, Jack.

Jack. Yes, I suppose you know all about it.

Dwarf. You should be more careful, Jack.

Jack. What do you mean ?

Dwarf. Go this way, Jack.

Jack. I've tried your ways before.

Dwarf. They were right.

Jack. Perhaps . . .

Dwarf. Goodbye, Jack, and good luck.

[*Disappears.*]

Jack. Oh, very well, I will go the way the little man has pointed. Perhaps the third time I shall be more fortunate. [*Looking across the stage.*] Who is there ? Hallo, friend. Are you in difficulty ?

[Traveller *enters.*]

Traveller. Yes, I want to get across this river.

Jack. I will help you. Here is a log of wood. I will throw it across. There, now step on to the end of it and reach across and hold my hand. There, now jump. Good. You are safely across. A pleasant journey to you. [*Turns to go away.*]

Traveller. Hi, not so fast. I must pay you for your kindness.

Jack. There is no need.

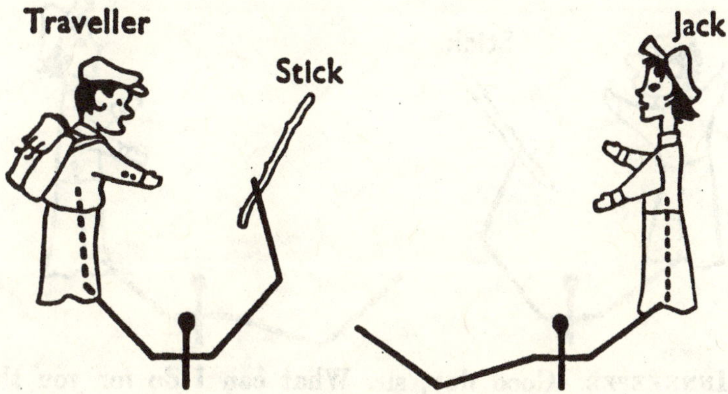

Traveller. But I will. I will tell you a secret. I am a magician. Here now is a stick which acts by itself. If anyone has done you a wrong, just say, "Up, stick and beat them." Then the stick will beat them until you tell it to stop.

Jack. Oh, thank you, oh, thank you. This is a wonderful gift. I am very pleased with it.

Traveller. Goodbye, Jack, and good luck. [*Goes out.*]

Jack. This is not a fortune, but it might win me one. Come, stick, let us be on our way. I wonder what happened to my donkey and my table. The donkey did give me gold and silver, and the table did give me a feast once. [*To audience.*] Do you know what can have happened to them?

[*Backchat with audience who will give him all the necessary information.*]

What! That innkeeper stole them from me. Then I will go straightway and have a few words with the old rascal. I will go right in and see the thief.

[*Goes off and comes on again.*]

Here is the inn, and there is the landlord.

[INNKEEPER *enters.*]

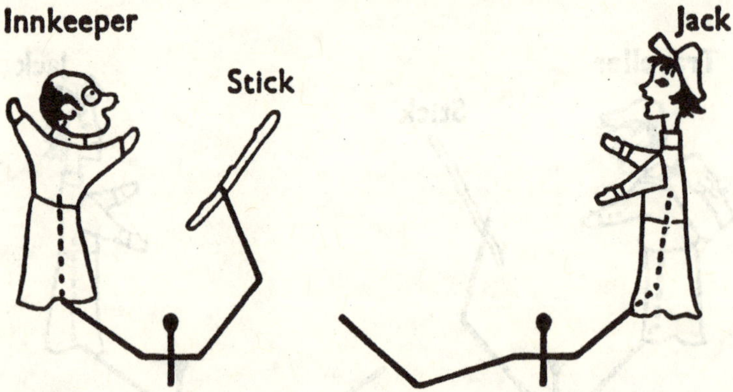

INNKEEPER. Good day, sir. What can I do for you this time ?

JACK. You can answer me a question.

INNKEEPER. What is it ?

JACK. Where are my donkey and my table ?

INNKEEPER. Sir, I am a poor but honest man.

JACK. Did you take my donkey and put another in its place ?

INNKEEPER. But, er, er . . .

JACK [*to audience*]. Did he ? [*To* INNKEEPER.] You hear what they say. Did you take my table and put another one in its place ?

INNKEEPER. I, er, er . . .

JACK [*to audience*]. Did he ? [*To* INNKEEPER.] You hear what they say. [*To audience.*] What do you think I had better do ?

[*The audience tells him.*]

Yes, a jolly good idea. Look, landlord. I have brought something else for you to steal. [*Whispers to stick.*] "Up, stick and beat him."

[*The stick beats the* INNKEEPER *who runs around shouting and trying to dodge it.*]

INNKEEPER. Your table is in the other room . . . your donkey is in the stable . . . take them and hurry . . . Call off this stick . . . take anything you want . . . O help . . .

[*He runs off with the stick after him.*]

JACK. Bravo, stick. You go on chasing him until I call you back. [*Goes out and comes in with the donkey.*] Here is my donkey. [*Goes out and comes in with the table.*] Here is my table. Come, Neddy, give me a lift with the table and let us be going.

[*Goes off singing.*]

[*Jack enters with donkey and meets his father. The stick need not appear until called for, as it has been left to chase the innkeeper.*]

FATHER. So you dare to come back here again.

JACK. Yes, and this time I have really brought my fortune with me. I am going to marry Jill and neither you nor anyone else is going to stop me.

FATHER. This looks like another donkey and another table. I hope they are better than the last ones you brought.

JACK. I will show you. This is Neddy. I will pull his ears, like that, and there is the gold and silver.

[*Gold and silver drop from the donkey's mouth.*]

FATHER. Eh what ! Gold and silver for pulling a donkey's ears !

JACK. And in case you are hungry, watch. "Table, be covered."

[*The table is covered.*]

FATHER. Eh what ! A feast, for just those words!

JACK. So I have my fortune and now I will marry Jill.

FATHER. Fortune, indeed! You are far too young and silly to own things like this. I will take care of them.

JACK. But they are mine. I earned them.

FATHER. Maybe, but I am going to look after them.

[*He takes the table away.*]

JACK. O, father, I haven't shown you the other thing I earned.

FATHER. Well, what is it? Show it to me.

JACK. Stick, come here! [*The stick appears.*] This is it. It is a magic stick.

FATHER. What can it do?

JACK [*to audience*]. Shall I show him? [*Backchat with audience.*] "Up, stick, and beat him."

FATHER. Ow, murder, help . . .

[*The stick beats him and chases him away.*]

JACK. Now at last, I can marry my Jill. [*Calling.*] Jill, Jill, where are you?

[JILL *enters.*]

Position of Puppets as on page 59

JACK. Come, Jill. I have my fortune now. A donkey which gives us gold and silver, a table which gives us a feast whenever we need it, and a stick to drive anyone away who tries to harm us. So now we can be married.

[*They kiss and sing.*]